THE WORLD UNDER MY FINGERS

PERSONAL REFLECTIONS ON BRAILLE

Edited by
Barbara Pierce

Table of Contents

INTRODUCTION

All parents yearn for their children to be happy and healthy and to grow up to live satisfying and productive lives. If it were possible to do so, we would arrange for them to be attractive, intelligent, ambitious, sensible, and funny—all the traits, in short, we wish we could boast and never have enough of, no matter how talented we are. Obviously our children do not grow up to exhibit all these traits, but most of them do well enough with the skills and attributes we do manage to impart to them.

Sometimes, however, a child must come to terms with very real difficulties: frequent or serious illness, mental handicaps of one kind or another, or physical disability. The parents, too, must then face the limitations or alterations that such problems place on our children and on our dreams for them. The natural instinct is to feel that the more closely the child can be taught to mimic the behavior of so-called normal youngsters, the better off he or she will be in the long run, because the differences will be less obvious. If we are honest with ourselves, we usually find that a part of this reaction also comes from the feeling that we will not have to confront the problem as directly and painfully if the trappings of disability are kept to a minimum.

However, successful adults who have coped with various disabilities for many years have a somewhat different notion. We have found that striving for the independence and richness of normal adult experience is far more satisfying and constructive than trying to use the methods of those who have no obvious disabilities, even though such striving requires mastery of alternative techniques and skills.

In the case of people whose vision is so poor as to make it difficult or impossible to read regular print for extended periods of time and to write accurately and legibly, it is extremely useful to learn to read and write using Braille. When learned early and taught by a knowledgeable teacher, Braille is an invaluable tool for those who cannot use print comfortably for extended periods of time or in all kinds of light.

Most of the following stories and articles are firsthand accounts of people who have depended on Braille all their lives or who were denied Braille instruction and have paid the price of that neglect for years. As you consider whether or not to ask that your child be taught Braille, we invite you to consider the experience and views of these competent blind adults.

Young as he is, Jeremy Lincicome already enjoys Braille

WHY LARGE TYPE?

The type size used in this book is 14 point for two important reasons: One, because typesetting of 14 point or larger complies with federal standards for the printing of materials for visually impaired readers, and we wanted to show you what type size is helpful for people with limited sight.

The second reason is that many of our friends and supporters have asked us to print our paperback books in 14 point type so they too can easily read them. Many people with limited sight do not use Braille. We hope that by printing this book in a larger type than customary, many more people will be able to benefit from it.

The simple pleasure of sitting quietly and reading a good book was long delayed for Barbara Pierce. She was denied Braille as a child so has had to teach herself to read as an adult.

AN OPEN LETTER TO PARENTS

By Barbara Pierce

Editor's note: Barbara Pierce is the President of the National Federation of the Blind of Ohio and Editor of the Braille Monitor magazine.

Can you remember the intoxication of learning to read? I can. When I began first grade, the Scott-Foresman primers about the adventures of Dick, Jane, and Sally were in use, and I still remember the picture of Dick standing on his shoulders in a pile of leaves, feet kicking in the air, while one of his sisters intoned the page's text, "Look at Dick! Funny, funny Dick!"

Had I but known it, those early weeks of first grade were the high point of my reading career. We gathered around the teacher in reading groups to sound out the words and falter our way through each page. I was good at it. I understood the principles of picking out the sound of each letter and shoving them together rapidly enough to guess at the meaning. The result was that I was in the first reading group.

My success didn't last long. By second semester each page bore many more lines of print, and my mother was forced to work with me at home after school or before bed to help me keep up. For I was what they called a low-vision child. I could see the print with only one eye, and I am certain that I was legally blind, though no one ever used that word in my hearing. Mother placed a little lamp close to the page so that I could see as well as possible, but the letters were still blurred, and I could never get the hang of reading an entire word at once.

By second grade I was in the second reading group, and by third grade I had slipped to the third group, despite the lamp now clipped to the side of my desk. I had to face the truth: I was dumb. I lay awake at night worrying about the increasing number of spelling workbook exercises left undone because my reading and writing were too slow to complete them in class. I still maintained an unbroken string of perfect spelling tests because my parents drilled me on the spelling lists every week. The tests were nothing, but the workbook! I fantasized about what it would be like to go to bed at night and not stare open-eyed into the black prospect of mortification when the truth about me and my incomplete work eventually came to my parents' notice.

It happened at the close of the third marking period, and it came, as such things do, like a bolt from the blue. I had actually brought home what I thought was a good report card—all A's and B's—except for art, penmanship, and gym, in which I always got C's. Everybody knew that I was terrible at those things because "Barbara's blind as a bat." But the dreaded unmasking of my shameful secret in the spelling workbook seemed to me to have remained hidden beneath an A for yet one more grading period. I handed my mother my report card and ran out to play. But when my brother and I were called in for dinner (Dad was out of town at the time), I knew that something was wrong; Mother had been crying, and she did not sit down to dinner with us. She said that she had a headache. It soon became apparent that I was the headache. My report card had betrayed me after all. In all that hard-to-read small print at the bottom the teacher had given me a U (unsatisfactory) in the puts-forth-best-effort category, where I was used to getting E's(Excellent) or at least S's (satisfactory).

Mother went to school the next day and learned the horrible truth about me. I was astonished to learn afterward that the relief of having my shameful secret out in the open actually reduced my burden. True, I had to make up all the work I had been avoiding because the reading had become too difficult. Play time was much reduced, and I had to learn all over again how to go to sleep without worrying, but things were never again as bad.

In the following years we tried magnifying glasses for my good right eye, and the summer after fourth grade I had to be tutored in an effort to learn to read with high magnification. In September of fifth grade my new teacher called on me to read a paragraph in the geography book during the class lesson. I read like a second grader, and I was mortified. The teacher never called on me again. By sixth grade I was hardly using the glasses at all. I was quick to learn as long as I didn't have to struggle to make sense of the print, and it was easier on everyone for the teacher to assign a rapid reader to work with me on in-class reading projects.

Finally, at the close of seventh grade, my parents faced the painful truth: if I were to have any hope of literacy, I would have to learn Braille. Print was no longer an option. I mastered the Braille code in a summer of weekly lessons taught by a woman who used Braille herself, though she admitted that she was not a good Braille reader. She assured me that her husband could read Braille rapidly, but I never heard him or anyone else use the code efficiently. People told me it was important to use my Braille and that practice would increase my speed. But by that point in my education I had already worked

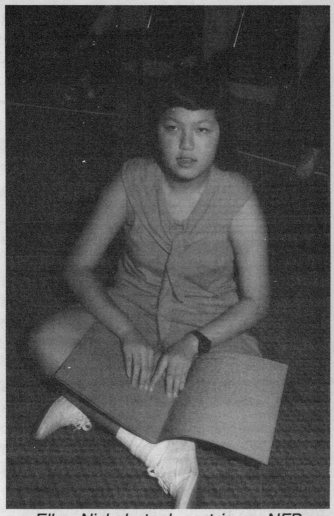

Ellen Nichols took part in an NFB fundraiser in which participants found sponsors for every Braille page read.

out alternative ways of getting my reading and writing done, and I was no longer eager to crawl down a page of text as we had done in early elementary school. I practiced writing Braille with my slate and stylus because I knew that in college I would need a good way of taking notes in lectures, but I never made time to learn to read Braille properly.

Now that I am a member of the National Federation of the Blind, I know hundreds of people who read Braille easily and well. Some of them could not see print when they were beginning school, so Braille was the only option for them. But many more could make out print when they were learning to read, even though as adults they cannot see it. They were lucky enough to be taught Braille along with print, and they simply and naturally learned to decide which method would be most useful for each reading task. As a result they now read Braille at several hundred words a minute.

I have never regretted learning to read print. Everyone should know the shapes of print letters, but I will always bitterly regret that I was not taught Braille as a small child. Today I am struggling to gain the speed and accuracy in reading Braille that I should have had by the time I was ten. I have now been working at it for six years, and my reading speed has tripled, but I must face the fact that I will probably never read as well as a bright ten-year-old. Setting aside the fact that the adult brain does not master new skills as rapidly as does a child's, I cannot bring myself to practice reading aloud to my long-suffering family. The time for taking advantage of such an opportunity is childhood, and I cannot inflict my stumbling reading on my husband.

If my mother could speak to you who are facing the dilemma of whether or not to demand that your children learn Braille, she would urge you to decide in favor of Braille. No matter how clearly a youngster can see print at the moment, if the vision is fragile or problematic in any way, Braille will often become invaluable in the future, even if print too continues to be useful. I urge you to keep your child's options open and your expectations high. All young things need space to stretch and grow within their God-given abilities. Please insist that your child be given a chance.

WHO SHOULD LEARN BRAILLE

Editor's note: The following is an excerpt from a document written by members of the National Federation of the Blind of Maryland and staffers from the Maryland Department of Education, which is titled "Selection of Reading and Writing Media for Students with Visual impairments: Braille, Print, or Both?"

Decision-Making Process

The decision to teach Braille, print, or both will take into consideration all of the information gathered during the assessment. The assessment information will help the team select from among the following options. Students may be taught to use:

1. Braille

2. Print

April and Amanda Jones from Tennessee are already learning and using Braille

3. Braille, complemented with print

4. Print, complemented with Braille

The remainder of this section provides examples of the kinds of assessment data that will assist a team in choosing one of the four options. Of course, assessment descriptions provided below are somewhat generic, i.e., not all parts of the descriptions will apply to each student. Since students are individuals, not everyone will fit neatly into one of the four categories. In reviewing these descriptions, team members should ask which factors best describe the individual student.

It is also important to remember that, when the selected option includes both Braille and print, the amount of use of one or the other will vary with each student. Student input should be obtained so that the team decision is sensitive to student preference and concerns. Additionally, as a student's vision or visual demands change over time, the use of one medium over another may change.

However, even though a student may use one medium more than another at a given time, it is critical that the student develop proficient use of both. For the preschool student this will mean that opportunities for visual and tactual activities are provided equally. Later, the amount of time teaching or practicing with a certain medium will depend on all assessment data and the current needs of the student. The team must continually focus on the ultimate outcome so that the student will be able to choose and use the medium of preference or the medium most functional for a given situation.

Which Students Should Learn Braille?

Medical Factors: Student is totally blind, nearly so, or expected to experience rapid loss of vision.

Physical Factors: An additional disability does not interfere with the ability to learn Braille.

Environmental Factors: Adjustments in natural and artificial lighting do not enhance student ability to read print.

Print Reading Factors: If the student can read print at all, reading is extremely slow and laborious, even when all print factors have been adjusted for maximum efficiency.

Handwriting Factors: Student cannot read own handwriting to carry out functional handwriting demands.

Low Vision Technological Factors: Student cannot read print at any comfort level, even using a CCTV or other non-portable devices.

Which Students Should Learn Print?

Medical Factors: Student has a stable eye condition or has a prognosis of continued improvement.

Physical Factors: Student experiences no fatigue or discomfort from reading. The nature of an additional disability prohibits tactual reading. Student, when systematically assessed, exhibits inability to process tactual information with any accuracy and facility.

Environmental Factors: Student does not require extensive modifications in natural or artificial lighting in order to read comfortably for extended periods of time.

Print Reading Factors: Student reads regular print comfortably and efficiently in most settings and circumstances. Reading rate accuracy is commensurate with student's expected grade level. Performance level is commensurate with overall ability. Student can use print easily for all academic, nonacademic, and vocational needs.

Handwriting Factors: Student has legible handwriting and can easily read own and others' notes at a comfortable distance, even after some time has elapsed.

Low Vision Technological Factors:

Student reads regular print without low vision devices and comfortably uses pocket-size magnification for reading fine print, such as the telephone book, medicine labels, dictionary, and encyclopedia.

Which Students Should Learn Braille Complemented with Print?

Medical Factors: Student has diagnosis or prognosis of severe visual impairment, has a degenerative eye condition, or has severely restricted visual fields.

Physical Factors: Student holds book close to face, can read only large print, or regularly suffers from headaches, fatigue, or visual discomfort after reading. Student exhibits strong preference for tactual exploration and learning. Student can read using an electronic low vision aid, but only with effort; cannot read with handheld magnifiers with any reasonable speed or comprehension. Student is unable to complete assigned school work in a timely manner consistently and independently.

Environmental factors: Glare and/or lighting variations make reading difficult or impossible in many settings.

Print Reading Factors: Student's print reading speed is far below that of other students of the same developmental level. Student consistently demonstrates inaccuracy when reading. Student has difficulty in reading a variety of print styles or print on colored background.

Handwriting Factors: Student can only read notes when written with a broad tip pen one to two inches high and may have difficulty accurately reading what was written or can only read notes using a CCTV or other non-portable device.

Which Students Should Learn Print Complemented with Braille?

Medical Factors: Student has a currently stable eye condition but is at risk of eventual deterioration, has a slowly progressive eye condition, has restricted visual field, or has fluctuating vision.

Physical Factors: Student's posture during reading results in back and neck strain or headaches. Student complains of watering eyes, blurring, or other visual discomfort after extensive reading or writing tasks. Student cannot complete assignments without relying on other individuals or technology for reading and/or note taking.

Environmental Factors: Glare and/or lighting variations make reading difficult or impossible in some settings.

Print Reading Factors: Student cannot read regular print easily and accurately for an appropriate length of time in order to complete tasks throughout the day. Student may read material in both regular and large print formats. Student reads primarily in large print format combined with optical or electronic low-vision devices. Student is unable to maintain a reading rate commensurate with grade level work demands. Student depends on extraordinarily large print for accessing practical information such as oral report notes, grocery lists, names and addresses, etc. In preschool observations should include how a student approaches learning, i.e., a visual versus tactual approach.

Handwriting Factors: Student has difficulty producing and reading own or others' handwriting.

Low Vision Technological Factors: Student may use CCTV or other non-portable devices for visual materials such as maps and diagrams.

Like many other parents, Marc Maurer, President of the National Federation of the Blind, enjoys reading to his children, David Patrick and Diana Marie. The youngsters are glad that their dad knows Braille.

KEEPING WITHIN THE LINES

by Marc Maurer

Editor's Note: Marc Maurer is President of the National Federation of the Blind. He is a graduate of Notre Dame and the University of Indiana Law School and a member of the bar of several states and the United States Supreme Court. He is also the father of two young children. Braille is an important tool for him—in his career and in his home. Here is what he has to say about some of his early experiences with Braille:

The kindergarten in the public school that I attended when I was five left me with a feeling of alienation and frustration—though I didn't know the words to describe the problem. My teacher was a kind and gentle lady, who tried to help me, but I presented difficulties which she felt unable to solve. Many of the kindergarten activities were done visually. Learning colors, drawing, recognizing letters and numbers, naming the geometric shapes—all of these were presented visually. Some kindergarten tasks could be done quite effectively without sight—counting, reciting the alphabet, remembering your own address and telephone number, listing in order the days of the week or the months of the year. But in the drawing classes I was unable to "keep within the lines," and "keeping within the lines" was important.

I learned the shapes of the print capital letters from the building blocks we had, and I came to know the forms of numbers in the same way. By the time kindergarten had come to an end, I had learned to print my name, M-A-R-C, but I usually got it backwards—C-R-A-M. As I viewed it, the experiment with kindergarten was only marginally successful. Although it was never stated, the lesson of kindergarten was unmistakable—blind people are different from others; they require kindness; they can't do the ordinary things that other people do; they can't keep within the lines.

My parents decided that I would attend the school for the blind even though doing so meant that I would be away from home during most of the school year. Of course, I could return home for holidays and during some weekends, but the rest of the time I would live in a dormitory with my classmates at the school. At the age of six I left home. The school for the blind was over a hundred miles from our house. It was the beginning of a different kind of life.

Because I was at that time almost totally blind, I was expected to learn Braille. We started the learning process with flash cards. There was a straight line of Braille dots across the top of each card and a single word in the center. I still remember the first flash card I ever read; it contained the word "go."

Each of us was given our first reading book—the primer about Dick and Jane and Spot. It was the first Braille book I ever had in my hands. My book seemed to be about a foot square and about a half an inch thick. The teacher told us to open our books to page one. My desk was in the first row, about the sixth or seventh from the front. The first child in the row was asked to read page one. When there were mistakes, the teacher corrected them.

Then the second student was asked to read the same page. Again, when there were mistakes, the teacher corrected them. The lesson continued in the same manner. Each student in the first row was asked to read page one. By the time the teacher got to me, my job was clear, and my performance flawless. With my fingers on the page, I spoke the words of page one with never an error or hesitation. The teacher praised me highly and asked me to come to the front of the room. She produced a gold star from her desk drawer and pasted it to page one of my book. She told me to take my book home and show it to my mother. This is exactly what I did. On Friday night after the journey home I proudly produced my primer, opened it to page one, and recited the words which appeared on the page.

My mother is a properly suspicious woman. She had learned Braille in the years before I attended school because she thought it might be helpful to me. She asked me if she could borrow the book, and of course I gave it to her. Later during the weekend she brought me a page of Braille and asked me to read it. Without much concern I confessed that I could not. My mother told me that it was an exact copy of page one of my book. I had memorized the words, but I was not able to read them.

During the summer between my first and second grade years, my mother took matters in hand. She told me that I must learn to read, and she said that she would teach me. For an hour every morning I was going to study Braille. I complained. The other kids got to go outside to play, but I could not. Nobody else had summer school at home—only me. But none of my griping did any good. My mother had made up her mind; I was going to learn to read.

When I returned to the school for the blind for second grade, I discovered the library of Braille books— that collection of sweet-smelling Braille volumes almost a foot square and about two and a half inches thick. During the next four years I read every book that the librarian would let me have. I developed the habit of reading at night. Blindness has some advantages. I would slide the book under the bed sometime during the evening. Bedtime was 8:00. The house parent made his rounds between 8:30 and 8:45. I could hear his shoes coming down the hall and then receding in the distance. When the footsteps had faded, the book came out. No light is needed for Braille. Sometimes it was cold, but the Braille book would fit under the covers.

I tried the same system at home, and it worked most of the time. When I got caught, which happened occasionally, my mother spanked me. The punishments were fair, but the reading was worth it.

Although I complained bitterly about learning Braille, I am deeply grateful to my mother for insisting that I learn it. How fortunate I am that she understood the necessity for me to read. How fortunate I am that she was persistent and demanding. How fortunate I am that she had learned Braille herself and was able to teach me.

Today we in the National Federation of the Blind do much to help make Braille available to blind students and to encourage the teaching of Braille both to children and adults who are blind. But this is not how it has always been. There was a time when Braille was regarded as inferior, and all too often today it does not get the attention it deserves. Much of my work as a lawyer could not have been done without Braille. I now read to my children most evenings. They enjoy the stories, and I enjoy the reading as much as they do. How different my life would have been without the ability to read Braille. How different it can be for the children of this generation if we give them the chance to learn. The message should not be that blind people are different and unable to take part. Even though I might not be able to draw, my mother felt certain that I could keep within the lines. We in the National Federation of the Blind are doing what we can to make it come true.

THE EVERYDAY USEFULNESS OF BRAILLE

by Lauren L. Eckery

Editor's note: We can hope that the time will come, sooner rather than later, when an article like the following will no longer be an appropriate candidate for inclusion in the pages of a publication like this. No one needs to persuade sighted people about the pervasive usefulness of print; the case has been made so effectively that even those for whom it is inconvenient, awkward, or painful struggle to use it. But would-be Braille-users and parents of children for whom print is not an efficient tool still need down-to-earth examples of the value of Braille in the conduct of everyday life. So here are some practical reminders about Braille from a busy, organized working woman and mother who uses Braille as efficiently and automatically as her sighted counterparts use print.

Lauren Eckery is an active working woman and mother. She frequently writes about her experiences as a blind person.

It is the early 1970's, and my family is traveling by car to Minnesota for a vacation. Both my mother and I like to read and crochet on long trips.

The dimness of the evening sky envelops us gradually, and my mother stops reading. She also decides she can no longer crochet. She wants to check the time but cannot see her watch without turning on the dome light. She chooses to listen to the radio or take a nap.

Meanwhile, in the back seat of the car, I continue my activities. I read my Braille magazine for a while. Then I crochet several rows on my afghan. Braille labels help me keep the different colors of yarn in order. Now and then I check the time on my Braille watch, the excitement mounting as we near our final destination.

It is the later 1970's or early 1980's. I am singing in my church choir. During our Thursday evening service prior to Good Friday, the lights are extinguished one by one until it is nearly dark in the sanctuary. While the choir sings, I notice a discreet scramble for notes and lyrics. I continue singing the alto part I have memorized and reading the lyrics in Braille. Rather than becoming anxious and embarrassed by struggling to continue the music, I go on as before, experiencing the special tone of the service.

It is any day. I am speaking to a group of school children, who are interested in what I am saying about blindness: "Given the proper training and opportunity, blind people can lead normal lives." But their favorite part of the presentation is the show-and-tell segment, during which I demonstrate various aids and appliances enabling the blind to be independent. Their greatest curiosity seems to revolve around Braille. "What is it? What do you do with it? How do you read and write it? Is it hard to learn?"

Simply telling the children that Braille is a blind person's equivalent to print is seldom enough. They seem to understand that Braille can be used in school for reading and taking notes, but for what else can one use it? Again, to oversimplify, saying that we use Braille for the same purposes one uses print for often goes uncomprehended. The children want concrete examples.

At our 1991 annual convention of the National Federation of the Blind, held in New Orleans, Louisiana, the usefulness of Braille was one of the underlying themes of our discussions. In the course of attending convention activities, I was observed and approached by several new Federation members who were losing some of their vision. They were grappling with the fact that they needed to learn Braille. Two young women who spoke with me knew that it made sense. They had been told that Braille could be useful to them, but they were reluctant to commit the full amount of time and effort necessary to learn Braille well enough to use it on a daily basis. Their lack of motivation seemed to stem from a lack of everyday examples in which using Braille could be useful and necessary for them. They, like the children I have spoken of previously, understood that Braille was useful for academic and employment pursuits, but what about blind people who are neither in school nor working? How could they make Braille such a part of their lives that they couldn't resist learning and using it efficiently? I was pleased to give these convention delegates concrete examples and encouragement in the use of Braille.

With the advent of our efforts to obtain a Braille bill in Nebraska, readers of *News from Blind Nebraskans* and other interested parties might appreciate some further examples of the everyday usefulness of Braille in the lives of everyday independent blind persons. Although the list is endless, here are some examples which have occurred to me during the writing of this article:

Taking telephone and other messages; making grocery and other lists; keeping telephone numbers, addresses, and other informational index files; placing Brailled clear plastic sheet overlays into printed children's books so that blind parents, teachers, and others can read to blind or sighted children; keeping recipes, crochet or knitting patterns, and instructions of various types in Braille for efficient and independent access--and the list goes on.

One can label almost anything in Braille: photographs; phonograph records; cassette tapes; video tapes; games; puzzle pieces; food items; medications; printed materials for later filing; checks; receipts; bills and other documents for independent handling of finances; household and other appliances; newsletter mailers; coupons; greeting cards; post cards; gift tags; yarn, thread, and other needlework equipment; etc.

At this point one might decide that such labeling mania is overwhelmingly time-consuming. Abbreviations to the rescue! For instance, when I label a spool of thread, I abbreviate the color so that the small label will fit on the end of the spool—"bl" for blue, "br" for brown, "bk" for black, "gy" for gray, "pk" for pink. Most blind people use a combination of memory, recognition by touch, sighted assistance, and Braille labeling for identification.

An especially interesting example of labeling comes from my storehouse of childhood memories. One of my favorite pastimes for most of my youth was cutting out and coloring paper dolls freehand. For several years I could see blobs of color well enough to use a color-coded system for naming my paper dolls ("Laurie" was blue skirt and white top, for example). As my vision waned and the diversity in the names I chose for these paper dolls increased, I eventually changed my naming system to one in which I wrote each doll's name in Braille on it. To this day, I have a collection of some of those paper dolls. My ten-year-old daughter, Lynden, has enjoyed looking at Mommy's collection. She has asked me the names of many of the dolls. Although I do still remember the names of some of the dolls with colored clothing by recognizing some other characteristic about them, reading the Braille names is foolproof. If I had wanted to continue coloring the dolls' clothing, I could have devised a labeling system for my crayons and paints, but at the time Braille was my preferred choice, whether I colored the dolls or not.

Years later, as a young adult, I took a cue from my creative childhood's adaptive technique. When I lost the slight amount of vision I had, it was simple and natural for me to separate my yarn colors into individual bags and place a Braille label in each one for identification. This method works well for multicolored crochet projects.

One who is just beginning to learn Braille might feel exhausted by this incomplete list of examples. But believe me, if one has no opportunity to learn or use Braille or if one is limited in his or her creative capacity in devising multiple practical applications of Braille, he or she can indeed be illiterate and unnecessarily dependent on others for assistance.

On the other hand, if we use Braille pervasively in our lives, we will become experts at reading and writing it just as print users do with print. One of Lynden's earliest and best methods for beginning to learn print, besides watching "Sesame Street," was reading labels and signs in her environment. Why not make Braille as normal a part of our environment?

The main purpose for passing a Braille bill in every state of the Union is to maximize the independence and equality of blind persons, be they children or adults. Now, who could in good conscience oppose adoption of a Braille bill once they truly understood the everyday usefulness of Braille?

BLUEPRINT FOR LEARNING?

by Stephen O. Benson

Editor's note: In many ways a great deal of progress has been made by blind people in recent times—more jobs, better special tools and equipment, increased understanding. But in at least one critical area blind children growing up today are being badly shortchanged in a way that was very nearly unheard of fifty years ago. In recent decades most blind children have not routinely been taught how to read and write Braille. Many of these children have now reached adulthood. I talk to them by the hundreds. Almost without exception they feel they were betrayed by their teachers and the other experts their parents trusted to plan their education. We as blind people should not have to fight for

Steve Benson works in public relations for the Harold Washington Public Library in Chicago. He is also a member of the Board of Directors of the NFB. Braille is a vital tool for him.

blind children to have the chance to learn to read and write Braille.

Parents expect schools to teach sighted children how to read and write, and there are laws requiring that it be done. We want the laws to protect blind children, too. But the experts often fight against such laws. They seem to think deciding whether to teach a blind child to read Braille is very complicated. The truth is that it is very simple. If a child can't see well enough to read print easily, Braille should be taught. But that is not what usually happens, and the blind child pays a heavy price for the rest of his or her life.

Steve Benson does public relations and public education for the Chicago Public Library. He was trained as a high school English teacher and taught for a number of years before becoming a Braille instructor and then an administrator of a private agency serving blind people. He has much personal and professional experience with Braille. This is what he has to say:

At one and a half years of age my eye condition was diagnosed as retinitis pigmentosa, which often results in total blindness. As I approached first grade, my doctors and teachers (the team of professionals) asserted that I should use my limited vision to its maximum for as long as possible. My family was directed to enroll me in what was then called "sight saving." Print was to be the medium by which I was to learn to read.

The sight saving classroom was equipped with the best technology of the day (1948): dark green chalkboards with yellow chalk, yellow paper with heavy green lines, indirect lighting, desks with adjustable work surfaces that allowed the student to bring reading and writing materials closer to the face, and typewriters with large print. Each student wore prescription lenses and had access to hand-held magnifiers. In addition we used large-print textbooks. In third grade we learned to type by the touch typing method.

In my case and in countless others, neither equipment nor teaching techniques would or could work. The techniques and the teachers' efforts were misapplied. The prescription for sight saving class was in error. From the first day of class my limited vision prevented me from reading effectively. Over the course of the next four and a half years my visual acuity decreased while the print I was expected to read became smaller.

I remember alternately gazing out the window and puzzling over a printed page. By fourth grade my teachers had to print out my classwork by hand, using large letters and india ink. With all of that I still felt as though I was reading grey print on grey paper. Yet I remained in sight saving class until the middle of fifth grade.

The toll I paid for the professionals' decisions was high. I dreaded reading; my confidence eroded; I feared blindness; I acquired bad reading habits that carried over into adulthood. I never checked a book out of the library. Why should I? I couldn't read it.

During the summer of 1952 the professionals finally admitted that print might not be the right way for me to be getting an education. In September of that year I was transferred to what we referred to as the blind school, where I began to learn Braille. It wasn't difficult. My teacher was competent. She knew Braille. She gave me positive encouragement. My reading and writing speeds were slow at first; however, as I gained proficiency and confidence, speeds increased. In January of 1953, at age eleven, I checked out and read a library book for the first time in my life. It was in Braille.

Over the last forty years teams of professionals have continued to make the same foolish and costly decisions, probably with greater frequency as the years have passed. As a member of the National Federation of the Blind Scholarship Committee, I have met an astounding number of high school and college students who, because they had some vision, were deprived of Braille or were discouraged from learning it without regard to whether the student could read print well enough to compete with sighted peers.

One scholarship applicant, not unusual, uses taped books and a closed circuit television magnifier. Under the best conditions she is able to read for only a minute at a time, and that with great discomfort. She is enrolled as a part-time student in a community college, partly because her vision doesn't allow her to meet the reading and writing demands of full-time status. She has asked to be taught Braille, but her family and the teams of professionals with whom she has worked have actively discouraged it.

Too many parents assume that the experts must know what's best, and will necessarily do what's best for the child. Those assumptions are often wrong and prove to be quite costly to the blind child.

"What's best for the child" is a catch phrase that too often translates into decisions that are convenient for the teacher, school, or district and into efforts to make the blind child's educational needs conform to budget priorities.

Were my experience forty years ago and that of the college student I described mere coincidence? I don't believe they were. Nor do I believe that de-emphasis on literacy (Braille) was or is accidental.

De-emphasis on Braille is disgraceful, just as de-emphasis on print would be. People who have a good command of reading and writing skills tend to do better in math, science, history, languages, music, and all the rest. People who can read and write successfully have a better chance at competitive employment and every other situation in life, for that matter.

The anti-literacy/anti-Braille position taken by so many educators of blind children and adults has had wider negative impact than they might imagine. Several years ago I worked at an agency for the blind in Chicago. In support of a program to teach Braille, I submitted a grant request to the Chicago Tribune Foundation. The grant request was turned down. The reasons, according to a foundation spokesman, were that Braille has nothing to do with literacy, it is obsolete, and reading can be done by recordings.

I was disappointed that the program did not receive that support. I was disgusted by the ignorance of the foundation personnel, but I was not surprised.

For fifteen years I taught Braille for the Veterans Administration at Hines Hospital. One of my assigned duties was to supervise Western Michigan University interns (student teachers) studying to become rehabilitation teachers.

An alarming number of these interns didn't know Grade II Braille, could not write with a slate and stylus, and had to be instructed in the use of an ordinary Braille writer. One intern didn't know Grade I Braille, though he had taken and passed a Braille course.

Though I wrote negative reports regarding their poor skills, all of these interns passed the internship, and presumably all were certified by the Association for the Education and Rehabilitation of the Blind and Visually Impaired (AER).

If future generations of blind people, children and adults, are to be literate, if future generations of blind people hope to be competitive in society, they must have access to the printed word by a method that will allow writing as well as reading. It is time for educators to grit their teeth and admit that a colossal error has been made.

Then they must bring themselves up to speed on Braille and all of its tools, mechanical and electronic. It is time for educators to join us in our effort to require that Braille be made available to any child who wants it and to participate in making sure that sufficient funding is available to make mandates and good intentions mean something.

Charlie Brown is a graduate of Harvard College and the Law School at Northwestern University. Today he is Assistant General Counsel of the National Science Foundation. He has always had and used a fair amount of residual vision, but he is also a committed Braille User.

BRAILLE MADE THE DIFFERENCE

Editor's note: Because I edit a monthly magazine, the Braille Monitor, *all kinds of material about blindness comes across my desk. But I recently read two articles within a two-hour period that, taken together, make the case for Braille more powerfully than anything I have yet seen or written. The pieces came from totally different sources, but the authors have a number of things in common. Both are working women—single, educated, committed to helping other people. Both live in the Midwest and were educated in regular schools. One, however, was taught Braille early and with wise insistence that she use it in her classes and at home. Her parents expected her to read well and did all the things that good parents do to encourage effective reading skills in their youngsters. The other was forced* to use print even when it was slow and painful. The cost academically and personally was immense. Not until she lost the remainder of her sight as an adult was she able to learn the Braille that she depends upon today and that could have made all the difference to her in school.

Mary Hartle lives in Iowa, though she grew up in Minnesota.

Jana Schroeder lives in Ohio. She was a 1984 NFB scholarship winner, and she has served as President of the National Federation of the Blind of the Miami Valley. She submitted her reflections on Braille as an essay in a Braille-writing contest conducted by the NFB of Ohio. Contest entries were to be written using a slate and stylus, and the winner received a Braille 'n Speak 640, a hand-held Braille computer. Jana's six-page essay was done in flawless Braille code without a single slate error. It was the winning *entry in the adult category. Viewed together, these two short autobiographies provide a powerful illustration in support of the contention that Braille is a vital tool for anyone who can't read print easily but who wishes to succeed in life. Here is Mary Hartle's article:*

The Value of Learning Braille as a Child

by Mary Hartle

Although visually impaired, I attended regular school in the 1950's and 1960's. I attended a parochial school in Minneapolis and was the only child with a vision impairment. I was taught to read print and progressed through the grades along with other children my age. No effort was ever made to teach me Braille. But, in retrospect, I wish I had been taught Braille as a small child.

Although I could read standard print, I could not read it as fast as sighted students could. My grades ranged from a few B's to several C's, and some D's. (My brothers and sisters got A's and B's.) I was tracked into the lowest-ability group in junior high, although I was promoted to the middle group halfway through both the seventh and eighth grades. I could not read as much material as others could and thus had to spend more time on homework. I also had to hold books much closer to my face. Due to prolonged periods of bending over to read books at close range, I developed posture problems which, to this day, require chiropractic treatment.

Learning became difficult and painful rather than joyful and exciting. As reading and learning became more difficult, I came to feel less intelligent. I began to feel shame and thus had more difficulty concentrating on learning. I became more anxious because of my increased difficulty. This was manifested in my struggles with arithmetic in fifth grade. I can still recall my extreme frustration and tears as I attempted to do my homework with my family's tutorial help.

As a child I read fewer books than my classmates, especially novels, although I did read magazines and a few quick-read books. I also had, and still have, trouble spelling many words because I was not able to see the letters within words correctly. For instance, spelling double-consonant words has been particularly difficult because my eyes did not focus normally when I first learned to spell these words.

Since I did not use Braille as a child, I was truly handicapped in my educational progress, and my self-confidence was low because I was unable to read fluently at a normal speed. I was embarrassed about both my slow reading speed and the fact that I had to look closer in order to read. Had I learned Braille earlier, I would have been able to read at a speed similar to that of sighted students.

As I progressed through high school and college, the reading requirements became much greater, and the size of the print became much smaller. In college I avoided classes with heavy reading demands, such as history and literature.

Over the past ten years I have lost the rest of my vision, thus necessitating my learning Braille. I am not unique. Many legally blind children with a little useful residual vision become blind adults with little or no ability to read print. Although I use Braille in my day-to-day life and on the job, I do not read with the speed I could have if I had learned Braille in the primary grades. There is nothing shameful about reading Braille or using any other non-visual technique. Today's blind children deserve a better education and a better chance to succeed in our highly competitive information age than I had. In fact, the need to read as efficiently as possible is more crucial today than ever before. Without Braille the chances of these children's getting through high school, much less going beyond it, will be minimal.

When I think of how much Braille would have enhanced my education even though I could read standard print at the time, I know how important Braille is for children today who can barely read standard print or who rely on large print. School does not have to be and should not be torture. I believe visually impaired children must be given the opportunity to learn Braille if:

1. they cannot read print at speeds comparable to that of their classmates;

2. they cannot hold reading material at a normal distance from their eyes; or

3. they cannot read print for long periods.

Braille is as effective a reading method as print is, and blind and visually impaired children have the right to become as literate as their sighted classmates.

That was Mary Hartle's description of growing up and being educated without an efficient tool for reading and writing. Contrast her experience with that of Jana Schroeder:

Braille is an Essential Part of My Life Because...

by Jana Schroeder

I was born with extremely limited vision to a family with no prior experience of blindness. It was the early 1960's, and we lived near Dayton, Ohio. Looking back, I recognize that I was lucky to have been born in that place and time and into a sensible, loving family. Without that fortunate combination of factors, my life might have been very different.

My family did a lot of reading aloud. From my earliest days I assumed that I would learn to read when I went to school, just as my sighted brothers had.

I began my education in a public school that included a resource room for blind students. These students were assigned to a regular classroom where we spent most of our time, but we went to the resource room for part of the day to learn the skills of blindness. I understand that Dayton was one of the first cities in Ohio with a public school program for blind children, beginning in the 1950's.

In the first grade, when reading lessons began in earnest, I was encouraged to read print. Various magnifiers were tried, but the only thing that worked for me was to put my nose against the paper and hope the print was big and dark enough. This worked fine with first grade primers. However, I quickly read all the big print picture books at the local library. My mom and I soon discovered that in second- and third-level books the print quickly diminished in size to the point where I could not distinguish the letters.

My mother believed, like most sighted people (at least those who are not blindness professionals), that blind people read Braille. So, sensibly, she insisted that I be taught Braille. Fortunately the resource room teachers agreed. I cannot be certain that it would be as easy if I were in school today. I believe that very few blind students in the Dayton area today are taught Braille.

I had heard my mom and other adults read quickly and fluently, and I assumed that I would read like that myself. I was never told that Braille was slower or harder than reading print. I simply accepted that I was learning to read with my fingers while my sighted classmates learned to read with their eyes.

One of the best things about the school I attended was that it had a Braille library. Never since then have I had access to a library where I could browse to my heart's content. I took home a different book almost every night. My favorites were biographies and the Little House series by Laura Ingalls Wilder. On the forty-five-minute drive to and from school I would often read aloud to Mom. She endured a lot of stumbling and mispronunciation with patience and good humor. From those earliest days I received a lot of praise from my parents, grandparents, and other people for my reading and writing ability. I knew that I read as well as or better than most of my classmates, and this knowledge helped lay a solid foundation of self-esteem that has served me well in the years since, when faced with new challenges.

In the fifth grade a significant challenge came along in the form of the slate and stylus. By this time I was attending school in my own district with an itinerant teacher who came to work with me a couple of times a week. She told me that I needed to learn to use the slate and stylus because I would soon be going to junior high and I couldn't lug a heavy, noisy Brailler with me from class to class.

I absolutely hated the slate. My *e's* and *i's* were inevitably transposed, and I invariably put the paper in crooked. I pretty much refused to practice, so my itinerant and classroom teachers got together and decided that I would be required to take spelling tests using the state and stylus. I always did well on my spelling tests, so I wasn't very happy with this new development. Gradually, however, I didn't have to reverse each letter consciously before writing it. My speed picked up, and my diagonal lines became horizontal. Since then I have written thousands of pages with the slate and stylus.

When I was in high school, closed circuit televisions began to become affordable and popular. It was very exciting to be able to read things that were only available in print, like the covers of my record albums. I spent one whole summer reading a 500-page novel that I could have read in about three days in Braille, because that was what all my friends were reading.

I knew, however, that the CCTV was no substitute for Braille. I'm almost glad that the CCTV was not available when I was in first grade because I don't know if Braille would then have been emphasized in my education. During my first two years in college my sight gradually decreased to the light perception I have today. Although I had to make some adjustments, already having well-developed Braille skills helped immensely.

In high school nearly all of my textbooks, including advanced math and French, were in Braille. In contrast, all of my college texts were on tape. By this time, though, I was familiar with spelling, punctuation, and the Braille literary and math codes. I took copious notes while listening to the texts and studied these at exam time rather than having to re-skim the entire book.

I have read that ninety-one percent of employed blind people know Braille. I am not at all surprised by this statistic. I am only surprised that so few educators and counselors of the blind seem to recognize the importance of Braille to employment. I cannot imagine being competitive without Braille.

Today I direct the Dayton criminal justice program of the American Friends Service Committee, a Quaker organization. My activities range from leading workshops and presentations in prison and the community to advocating for criminal justice reform. I use Braille every day to keep track of phone numbers, file away relevant statistics, make outlines for talks, draft articles, and much more.

Like most non-profits, we have a very small staff in our office. For the most part we do our own filing, typing, and minute-taking. My independence is greatly enhanced by the use of a scanner and other adaptive computer technology, but I don't think it would be possible for me to do my job at all without Braille. At meetings, workshops, and presentations I always have my slate and stylus ready. Although prison officials sometimes worry that my stylus could be turned into a weapon, I always have my Braille notes with me and have given several impromptu Braille lessons to interested prisoners.

Since those early days Braille has opened many doors for me. Reading is a source of great pleasure as well as information and education. Braille writing allows me not only to keep track of personal information but also to articulate and craft my thoughts into written communication that can be shared with others. I cannot imagine my life without Braille.

I am currently studying to become certified as a Braille transcriber and proofreader. I am deeply concerned by the lack of Braille skills among the blind today and the shortage of qualified Braille teachers, both for blind children and for people who become blind later in life. Perhaps someday I will have the opportunity to put my love of Braille to good use by teaching others to read it.

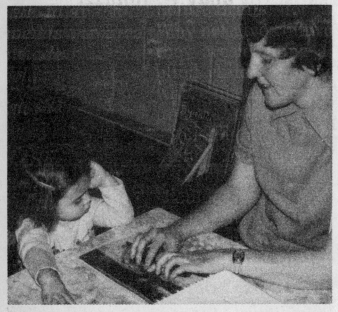

*Sandra Wright is a teacher from Iowa;
when she reads aloud to children, she
uses Braille*

BRAILLE OR PRINT: WHY THE DEBATE?

by Jody W. Ianuzzi

Editor's note: Let us begin by conceding that there really are some legally blind children who are appropriately being taught to read print. If the child can truly engage in sustained reading of normal print in most light with comfort, and if the strong likelihood is that the youngster's vision will remain stable, there is no sensible argument for insisting that Braille be taught unless the child or parents wish to have it done. But there are thousands of blind adults today (and our numbers are growing) who deeply regret that no one required us to learn Braille at a period in our lives when mastering it would have been relatively easy.

Many parents and children, wrestling with the denial that is an inevitable

*part of coming to terms with signifi-
cant vision loss, cling to the presence
of whatever tiny amount of residual
sight there may be as an indication
that their worst fears at least have not
come to pass. To the public mind
blindness is synonymous with helplessness, hopelessness, and incompe-
tence. Facing their children's blindness for the first time, parents, who
are after all members of the general
public, can be forgiven for reacting
out of ignorance and on incorrect information.*

*The betrayal of blind children that is
harder for knowledgeable blind
adults to forgive is that of many special education teachers who should
know better. But even here we must
remember that they too are the prod-
uct of their past inadequate education
and their current environment. These
educators are not the first professionals to confuse correlation with causa-
tion: given a choice between learning*

print and Braille, children with residual sight will usually choose print. The conclusion to which virtually every teacher incompletely trained in Braille is eager to jump is that the cause of this behavior is the difficulty and complexity of Braille. Or again, offered the chance to be excused from doing assignments in Braille, blind children will almost always opt for less work. The conclusion is that Braille is slow and inefficient. The actual cause in both these examples is that blind youngsters are normal kids, who like to be a part of the gang and who are delighted to get out of homework whenever possible.

A little honest reflection about this situation suggests that the real culprit here is the inadequate and inappropriate education of the special education teachers, most of whom are not competent or confident themselves in using Braille and who also believe that their students should not be ex-

pected to compete successfully in school or in life.

We of the National Federation of the Blind know just how damning and demeaning such a wholesale dismissal of blind students really is. There are too many studies of children's conforming exactly to their teachers' expectations for us to observe this phenomenon with unconcern. Recognition of what is happening to today's blind students fuels the Federation's state-by-state effort to require teacher competence in Braille reading and writing for those educators devoting their careers to teaching blind and visually impaired students. We must take every opportunity to educate and encourage good teachers about what they can do to assist and support their blind students, and we must confront those who would dismiss our efforts to improve the educational possibilities for these youngsters.

Jody Ianuzzi is the President of the Monadnock Chapter of the National Federation of the Blind of New Hampshire. She knows first-hand about limited opportunities and disappointed expectations. She is articulate and outspoken, and her message is compelling. Here is what she has to say about teaching Braille to children with a little residual vision:

Literacy has become a fashionable issue in the United States today. So many people have slipped through the educational system unable to read that it has become an embarrassment to their educators. Most of these people hid their illiteracy from their teachers or simply dropped out of school at an early age. This situation exists all across the country, but what about the one student population illiterate due to the decisions and actions of their teachers? These students are the blind children of America.

I would like to address the resource and itinerant teachers with the adult voice of their students:

I consider myself to have been functionally illiterate for most of my life! When I was growing up as a blind child in the public school system in Connecticut, I didn't have to learn Braille; I could read print. I was a high partial, and with my nose in the book I could read my first grade primer. It was work, but I could make out the letters. By the fourth grade the print began to get smaller, so I had to try even harder. In the seventh grade I was assigned to remedial reading classes because my reading speed was still at the third grade level. In high school I got all my work done; it just took me four times as long as my classmates. I loved learning, and I wove wonderful dreams for myself of academic success after high school.

I went off to college, but instead of succeeding, I fell flat on my face! There was no way I could keep up with the work load using the reading skills I had been taught. My totally blind friends had little trouble taking notes, reading, organizing their readers, etc. I told myself that I should have done better than they; after all I had some vision. But the fact was that I couldn't study as a sighted student, and I didn't have the skills to study as a blind one.

When I was a child, I had an itinerant teacher. She came to visit once or twice a week to help me with my class work and to evaluate my progress. I remember that she spent the majority of her time tutoring me when I fell behind. My mother was upset because the totally blind students always had priority over the partials. We got the teacher's leftover time. We weren't really blind, but we weren't really sighted either.

I am thirty-eight years old, and I am now learning Braille. It isn't a difficult task; memory is reinforced by using the signs. I love Braille! My reading time and speed are not limited as they are in print. I find Braille to be a refreshing experience with endless possibilities.

Reading print has always been like trying to listen to music on a distant radio station: the sound is so faint and there is so much static that it is hard to appreciate the music itself because listening is so much work. Reading Braille is more like sitting in a symphony hall. The music fills you without your even having to work. My well-meaning teachers thought they had made the right decision for me. Oh how I wish I had learned Braille as a child.

My story is not unique or exceptional. Hundreds, perhaps thousands, of blind adults now recognize that they missed out on a proper education. Perhaps this is because the retrolental fibroplasia generation (people born prematurely after World War II and exposed to too much oxygen in incubators) was the first to attend public school in numbers, and the methods of educating blind children who did not attend residential schools had not been established. Itinerant teachers of blind children were pursuing a brand new specialty. Now the next generation of blind students is attending public school, but the methods of teaching them haven't improved over the years. Instead, some of the misguided attitudes and ideas that were born in the infancy of this new profession have been institutionalized as established methods. When I was a student, fifty-two percent of blind students were learning Braille; now less than ten percent of blind children are doing so. Clearly illiteracy is increasing.

I was recently a speaker at a conference for itinerant teachers of blind children, where I attended a seminar on the subject, Braille or print for low vision students. I left this seminar feeling bitter, not for my own experience (I am changing that), but for the blind children of today. There are blind children with less vision than I have who are being taught print only. Their teachers believe that they are making the right decision. These children will be able to get by using their vision, but they will never be able to compete successfully with their peers.

The impression I got from listening to these teachers of blind children is that they perceive Braille to be a difficult system to learn. Imagine what would happen if music teachers decided not to teach their students to read music because they had come to believe that musical notation was too difficult to learn, much less to teach. How much music would students learn to play if their music teachers couldn't read the notes? Unfortunately, not very many teachers of blind children are fluent in reading and writing Braille themselves. No wonder so few blind youngsters are mastering the code.

Blind children are like all others; they don't want to appear different. If they are given a choice, they prefer print because their friends read print. But a low-vision child already looks different while struggling to read with his or her nose inching across the page, collecting printer's ink. Wouldn't teachers do better helping to instill confidence in their blind students as competent Braille readers instead of insisting that they become poor print ones? Sighted children are delighted to learn about Braille, but they have little understanding or compassion for the poor print reader, who can't keep up with them. The sooner the blind child realizes that it is no big deal to be different, the easier his or her life will be.

At this conference I was also told that the low-vision child might not want to learn Braille and that it is impossible to teach these kids what they don't want to learn. Suppose a sighted child didn't want to learn print, or the music student didn't want to learn musical notation; what would the teacher's response be? How much can any children be expected to learn if they are permitted to impose their own preferences on their early instruction in the fundamentals?

I believe that unconsciously teachers of blind students give children a choice posed like this: which will it be, the easy, acceptable, right way to learn, using print, or the difficult, different, old-fashioned way of reading, using Braille? Given any choice in the matter at all, which would any child select? Why can't teachers make Braille special in a positive way?

Braille was originally based on a system devised by the French army to send secret messages at night. The night writing was later perfected by Louis Braille for use by the blind. Why not give children the feeling that they are learning a secret code? The blind child can read in many places where his or her sighted friends can't: under the covers without the use of a flashlight, in the car traveling at night. You can read Braille books without people reading over your shoulder. You can even read your Braille book in your desk without your teacher knowing it. Why not make Braille fun!

The debate at this conference included discussion of the question whether or not a blind child could learn print and Braille at the same time. Wouldn't the child become confused? But the two systems don't compete for the same space in the brain. Can a child learn to use a calculator and a touch telephone at the same time? The two keyboards are reversed, but children don't find this confusing. The child knows that one is a phone, the other a calculator. I know a two-year-old who is learning English and German from her bilingual parents. She is having no difficulty learning the differences. If children can learn these things simultaneously, why should educators draw the line at learning Braille and print at the same time?

Many teachers believe that there are so many new high-tech aids available for blind children that it is no longer necessary to teach them the out-dated system of Braille. But how practical are some of these expensive, bulky devices like the closed circuit television when a child has to use it in a very limited and special environment? Will such devices be useful for obtaining all the information the child needs? Braille is portable, light-weight, and versatile.

The slate and stylus and the Brailler are simple, low-tech devices, but if you want to consider high-tech, portable equipment, the Braille 'n Speak and the Braille Mate are excellent note-taking and computer interface devices. These aids were never mentioned at this conference. The only aids discussed were those that depended on some limited sight.

There are many tools available for use by blind people, and none should be relied on exclusively or ignored. Each has its own place. Just as a carpenter needs many tools to build a house, a blind person can use many tools to acquire information. The Optacon, for example, is a slow but useful device for reading mail, and there are many other technical aids to assist a child who cannot use print efficiently and comfortably. But just as a carpenter can't be expected to build a house using only a hammer, no one tool should be used as the single device to help a blind child.

Conducting an evaluation to determine the reading method for a child is usually done under ideal reading conditions and in short periods of time. Is it reasonable to expect that a child will always have ideal lighting for reading and writing? How long can the child read before headaches or eye strain make it impossible to continue? Does the eye strain of reading contribute to increased eye problems? For example, when I was growing up, we didn't realize that my straining to read was inducing acute glaucoma attacks which have further decreased my vision. First and foremost a reading method should be comfortable and enjoyable to the reader. How much would you read if it always hurt or was always work?

When selecting a reading method, it is natural to think of the primary use to which we put it, reading books. But there are many other applications for reading and writing that have to be considered in choosing the most efficient method. Taking notes in class, doing research, labeling, maintaining recipes, filing addresses: these are all examples of the way we use reading. Thus, someone who can read print to a limited degree might not use print for note taking because of the amount of time it takes to write legibly or to decipher the notes later. In this example Braille would be faster. Labeling in Braille is more practical in many cases simply because it is impossible to get close to the labeled items to see them or to shine enough light on the print to read it—the back of an appliance or an array of canned goods on a storage shelf, for example. Blind children may not be dealing with these problems now, but they will as adults. The very purpose of education is to prepare youngsters for what they will face in the future!

One can reasonably ask whether today's older blind students are being taught how to order their own books from Recording for the Blind and whether they are learning to hire, supervise, and use readers for study and research in preparation for college. Blind students must know how to balance their schedules to accommodate their special study needs, whatever they happen to be. If blind students are to compete successfully in college and in life, all these are necessary skills.

I told conference participants about my experience as a low-vision student and about how I was learning Braille as an adult. Without thinking of the implications of her statement, one itinerant teacher turned to me and said, "If you're learning Braille, then good luck!"

Too many teachers of the visually impaired are limited by their own visual perception of the world. If they woke up tomorrow with low vision, many would try to funnel all the information they need through woefully inefficient eyes rather than learning to maximize their unimpaired senses. It is past time for them to think blind and not be limited by their vision.

If I could speak directly to open-minded teachers, I would say to them: when you evaluate your students, don't just think of how they are coping at the present; think ahead. What will happen to your students in college and as adults? Are you giving them all the skills they need to prosper in life, or will they have to be content with just getting by? Remember, if that is their fate, it will not have been because of their blindness but because they lacked the skills they needed to conduct their lives effectively as blind people. Ask yourselves this question: in twenty years will your students be grateful to you for teaching them the skills they needed, or will they be learning them on their own and trying to make up for lost time?

THE CHANCE TO READ

by Eric Duffy

Editor's Note: Eric Duffy is Director of Field Services for the National Federation of the Blind of Ohio. He and his wife Tracy live in Columbus and are expecting their first child. Braille is deeply important to both the Duffys, but there was a time when it looked as though Eric would be denied the right to learn it. Here is his story:

As a young child I enjoyed being read to. Whenever I could persuade anyone to sit down with me and a book, I was delighted. I particularly remember *Peter Rabbit*; *The Cat in the Hat*; and of course the classic, *Mother Goose*. When we were very small, my little sister Barb and I would pick up our books and pretend that we were reading. Sometimes we read to ourselves, and sometimes we

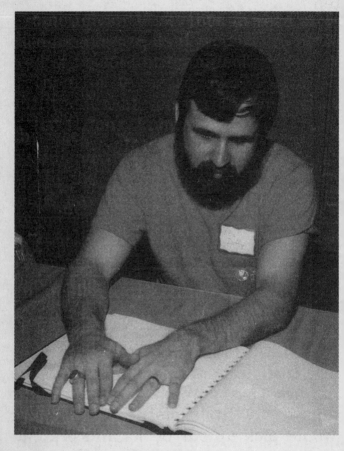

*Eric Duffy finds Braille indispensable.
He uses it every day in his work.*

read aloud to anyone who would listen.

I memorized things quickly, so pretending to read was easy for me. Barb could pick up any book and, by looking at the pictures, tell the story. I knew, however, that it wouldn't be long before Barb would no longer be pretending. She would be able to read books, newspapers, and everything else—just as the rest of our family could.

Eventually the day came when Barb began to read. She began to recognize the letters of the alphabet and then to sound out words. That is when I began to recognize that my blindness really might be a problem. I was the big brother, and I should have started reading before she did. I began asking my parents a lot of questions: how am I going to read? Am I going to go to school?

My parents explained that I was going to go to a special school for blind children. They said that I would learn to read and write Braille. Of course, I had no idea what Braille was. In order to give me some notion of the code, my mom punched small holes into a sheet of paper with a pencil. Obviously, these holes made no sense to either of us, but at least I was comforted by the knowledge that I was going to learn to read.

The time came when my mother took me to the Ohio State School for the Blind. I was given a variety of tests, most of which I do not remember. However, what my parents and the school officials did with the results of these tests might well, under other circumstances, have had a dramatically negative effect on the rest of my life. Because I have mild cerebral palsy, my parents were told that I would probably never learn to read and write Braille.

But when I started school, I did not know that I was not supposed to be able to read and write Braille. No one bothered to tell me what I could not or would not want to do, and I can only assume that my first-grade teacher chose to ignore the pronouncements of the experts. She simply gave me the opportunity to learn to read and write with the rest of my class. I started school in April, and by June I was reading and writing as well as anyone else in my class.

Today I use Braille in every aspect of my life. At home I label food items, cassettes, and compact discs. Braille reading is essential for playing board games such as Scrabble and card games such as Euchre. On the job I use Braille for note taking, writing down telephone numbers, and labeling file folders. I cannot even begin to name all the ways in which I use Braille at home and on the job.

Today I take my ability to read and write Braille for granted. But it frightens me to realize that I was almost denied the opportunity to learn it. What follow are the comments of the clinic evaluation team of the Ohio State School for the Blind: "Eric was a very cooperative boy who had difficulty walking. Although he has some vision, it does not appear to be adequate for reading any fine print. Developing usable Braille skills may be rather difficult for Eric because of his poor manipulative skills. His chief channel of learning will most likely be the auditory channel. Eric exhibits readiness for a beginning program for visually handicapped children."

Educational Specialist

This evaluation almost led to my not learning Braille. I know for certain that there are blind students today who are not learning Braille because of evaluation results like mine. My plea to parents and educators alike is this: give your children a chance to learn Braille. It is better to err on the side of Braille instruction than to deny any child the opportunity to read.

Dr. Kenneth Jernigan has read Braille since he was a small child. He is a dynamic public speaker using Braille text, but when he reads silently, his rate is more than 400 words a minute.

REFLECTIONS OF A LIFELONG BRAILLE READER

by Kenneth Jernigan

Editor's note: Kenneth Jernigan is the President Emeritus of the National Federation of the Blind. He has dedicated his life to improving the lives of blind people in this country and around the world. He is also a voracious reader. I have seen him pace a room, reading Braille aloud to his listeners. I have watched him scan Braille material at an unbelievable speed and read silently far faster than he could speak. In short, Braille is for him as useful a tool as print is to his sighted wife. How did he develop such excellent Braille skills? He read as a small child, read as much and as often as he could, and he kept on reading as he grew up. In short, he became a good reader in the same way that print readers become proficient. The following are some of Dr. Jernigan's recollections of his early days as a reader:

When I was a boy growing up in Tennessee, Braille was hard to come by. At the Tennessee School for the Blind (where I spent nine months of each year) Braille was rationed. In the first grade we were allowed to read a book only during certain hours of the day, and we were not permitted to take books to our rooms at night or on weekends. Looking back, I suppose the school didn't have many books, and they probably thought (perhaps correctly) that those they did have would be used more as missiles than instruments of learning if they let us take them out.

When we advanced to the second grade, we were allowed (yes, allowed) to come down for thirty minutes each night to study hall. This was what the "big boys" did. In the first grade we had been ignominiously sent to bed at seven o'clock while our elders (the second and third graders and those beyond) were permitted to go to that mysterious place called study hall. The first graders (the "little boys") had no such status or privilege.

When we got to the third grade, we were still not permitted to take books to our rooms, but we were allowed to increase our study hall time. We could actually spend a whole hour at it each night, Monday through Friday. It was the pinnacle of status for the primary grades.

When we got to the intermediate department (the fourth, fifth, and sixth grades), we were really growing up, and our status and prestige increased accordingly. We were allowed (I use the word advisedly—"allowed," not "forced") to go for an hour each night Monday through Friday to study hall, and during that time we could read books and magazines to our hearts' content. True, the choice was not great—but such as there was, we could read it. Of course we could not take books to our rooms during the week, but on Friday night each boy (I presume the girls had the same privilege) could take one Braille volume to his room for the weekend.

Before I go further, perhaps I had better explain that comment about the girls. The girls sat on one side of the room, and the boys sat on the other; and woe to the member of one sex who tried to speak or write notes to a member of the other. Girls, like Braille books, were difficult to get at—and all the more desirable for the imagining. But back to the main thread.

As I say, each boy in the intermediate department could check out one Braille volume on Friday night. Now, as every good Braille reader knows, Braille is bulkier than print; and at least four or five Braille volumes (sometimes more) are required to make a book. It is also a matter of common knowledge that people in general and boys in particular (yes, and maybe girls, too) are constantly on the lookout to beat the system. What system? Any system.

So on Friday nights we boys formed what would today be called a consortium. One of us would check out volume one of a book; the next, volume two; the next, volume three; et cetera. With our treasures hugged to our bosoms we would head to our rooms and begin reading. If you got volume three (the middle of the book), that's where you started. You would get to the beginning by and by. Now girls and Braille books were not the only items that were strictly regulated in the environment I am describing. The hours of the day and night fell into the same category. Study hall ended at 8:00, and you were expected to be in your room and in bed by 9:40, the time when the silence bell rang. You were also expected to be trying to go to sleep, not reading.

But as I have said, people like to beat the system; and to us boys, starved for reading during the week, the hours between Friday night and Monday morning were not to be wasted. (Incidentally, I should say here that there were usually no radios around and that we were strictly forbidden—on pain of expulsion and God knows what else—to leave the campus except for a brief period on Saturday afternoon—after we got big enough, that is, and assuming we had no violations on our record which required erasure by penalty.) In other words the campus of the Tennessee School for the Blind was what one might call a closed ecology. We found our entertainment where we could.

Well, back to Friday night and the problem of the books. Rules are rules, but Braille can be read under the covers as well as anywhere else; and when the lights are out and the sounds of approaching footsteps are easy to detect, it is virtually impossible to prohibit reading and make the prohibition stick. The night watchman was regular in his rounds and methodical in his movements. He came through the halls every sixty minutes on the hour, and we could tell the time by his measured tread. (I suppose I need not add that we had no clocks or watches.)

After the watchman had left our vicinity, we would meet in the bathroom and discuss what we had been reading. We also used the occasion to keep ourselves awake and exchange Braille volumes as we finished them. It made for an interesting way to read a book, but we got there—and instead of feeling deprived or abused, we felt elated. We were beating the system; we had books to read, something the little boys didn't have; and we were engaged in joint clandestine activity. Sometimes as the night advanced, one of us would go to sleep and fail to keep the hourly rendezvous, but these were minor aberrations—and the weekend was only beginning.

After breakfast on Saturday morning some of us (not all) would continue reading—usually aloud in a group. We kept at it as long as we could, nodding off when we couldn't take it any more. Then we went at it again. Let me be clear. I am talking about a general pattern, not a rigid routine. It did not happen every weekend, and even when it did, the pace was not uniform or the schedule precise. We took time for such pleasantries as running, playing, and occasional rock fights. We also engaged in certain organized games, and as we grew older, we occasionally slipped off campus at night and prowled the town. Nevertheless, the reading pattern was a dominant theme.

Time, of course, is inexorable; and the day inevitably came when we outgrew the intermediate department and advanced to high school—seventh through twelfth grades. Again it meant a change in status—a change in everything, of course, but especially reading. Not only could we come to study hall for an hour each night Monday through Friday and take a Braille volume to our room during weekends, but we could also check out Braille books whenever we liked, and (within reason) we could take as many as we wanted.

Let me now go back once more to the early childhood years. Before I was six, I had an isolated existence. My mother and father, my older brother, and I lived on a farm about fifty miles out of Nashville. We had no radio, no telephone, and no substantial contact with anybody except our immediate neighbors. My father had very little formal education, and my mother had left school just prior to graduating from the eighth grade. Books were not an important part of our family routine. Most of the time we did not have a newspaper. There were two reasons: our orientation was not toward reading, and money was scarce. It was the early thirties. Hogs (when we had any) brought two cents a pound; and anything else we had to sell was priced proportionately.

I did a lot of thinking in those preschool days, and every time I could, I got somebody to read to me. Read what? Anything—anything I could get. I would nag and pester anybody I could find to read me anything that was available—the Bible, an agriculture yearbook, a part of a newspaper, or the Sears Roebuck catalog. It didn't matter. Reading was magic. It opened up new worlds.

I remember the joy—a joy which almost amounted to reverence and awe—which I felt during those times I was allowed to visit an aunt who had books in her home. It was from her daughter (my cousin) that I first heard the fairy stories from *The Book of Knowledge*—a treasure which many of today's children have unfortunately missed. My cousin loved to read and was long suffering and kind, but I know that I tried her patience with my insatiable appetite. It was not possible for me to get enough, and I always dreaded going home, finding every excuse I could to stay as long as my parents would let me. I loved my aunt; I was fascinated by the radio she had; and I delighted in her superb cooking—about the key attraction was the reading. My aunt is long since dead, and of course I never told her. For that matter, maybe I never really sorted it out in my own mind, but there it was—no doubt about it.

As I have already said, I started school at six—and when I say six, I mean six. As you might imagine, I wanted to go as soon as I could, and I made no secret about it. I was six in November of 1932. However, school started in September, and six meant six. I was not allowed to begin until the next quarter —January of 1933.

You can understand that, after I had been in school for a few weeks, I contemplated with mixed feelings the summer vacation which would be coming. I loved my family, but I had been away from home and found stimulation and new experiences. I did not look forward to three months of renewed confinement in the four-room farm house with nothing to do.

Then I learned that I was going to be sent a Braille magazine during the summer months. Each month's issue was sixty Braille pages. I would get one in June, one in July, and one in August. What joy! I was six, but I had learned what boredom meant—and I had also learned to plan. So I rationed the Braille and read two pages each day. This gave me something new for tomorrow. Of course I went back and read and re-read it again, but the two new pages were always there for tomorrow.

As the school years came and went, I got other magazines, learned about the Library of Congress Braille and talking book collection, and got a talking book machine. By the time I was in the seventh grade, I was receiving a number of Braille magazines and ordering books from three separate regional libraries during the summer. Often I would read twenty hours a day—not every day, of course, but often. I read *Gone With the Wind*, *War and Peace*, Zane Grey, Rafael Sabatini, James Oliver Curwood, and hundreds of others. I read whatever the libraries sent me, every word of it; and I often took notes. By then it was clear to me that books would be my release from the prison of the farm and inactivity. It was also clear to me that college was part of that program and that somehow I was going to get there. But it was not just escape from confinement or hope for a broader horizon or something to be gained. It was also a deep, ingrained love of reading.

The background I have described conditioned me. I did not feel about reading the way I see most people viewing it today. Many of today's children seem to have the attitude that they are "forced," not "permitted," to go to school—that they are "required," not "given the privilege and honor," to study. They are inundated with reading matter. It is not scarce but a veritable clutter, not something to strive for but to take for granted.

I don't want children or the general public to be deprived of reading matter, but I sometimes think that a scald is as bad as a freeze. Is it worse to be deprived of books until you feel starved, for them or to be so overwhelmed with them that you become blase about it? I don't know, and I don't know that it will do me any good to speculate. All I know is that I not only delight in reading but believe it to be a much neglected joy and a principal passport to success, perspective, civilization, and possibly the survival of the species. I am of that group which deplores the illiteracy which characterizes much of our society and distinguishes many of its would-be leaders and role models. I am extremely glad I have had the opportunity and incentive to read as broadly as I have, and I believe my life is so much better for the experience that it borders on the difference between living and existence.

For Dr. Fred Schroeder, Braille is now an indispensable tool in both his personal and public lives.

BRAILLE TODAY AND TOMORROW

by Fredric F. Schroeder

The following is an excerpt from an address delivered at the annual conference of the California Transcribers and Educators of the Visually Handicapped, March 14, 1992, by Fred Schroeder, then Director of the New Mexico Commission for the Blind and President of the International Council on English Braille and now Commissioner of the U.S. Rehabilitation Services Administration. Dr. Schroeder is one of the most knowledgeable and influential figures in the field of work with the blind. Here in part is what he said to teachers and Braille transcribers in the spring of 1992; it is still relevant:

Much is happening nationally and internationally concerning Braille. Certainly we live in a time when it is getting more emphasis, which has resulted in greater availability and increased attention to instruction. We must recognize what is cause and what effect. When discussing Braille, it is easy to focus on the changes that have taken place. But all of this increased attention is the natural outgrowth of a growing conviction that literacy represents perhaps the most necessary tool if blind people are to live full and productive lives. In other words, the desire of and for blind people to function on terms of equality has driven the move toward recognizing Braille literacy as a vital step toward their meaningful integration.

The activity surrounding Braille is in many respects dramatic and encouraging. Here in the United States the Braille literacy movement can be seen in many ways. Today ten states [the number has now risen to twenty-five] have adopted Braille bills—a public policy statement about the legitimate role of Braille as a literacy tool for the blind. Five years ago, when the first Braille bill was introduced, the idea was controversial and sparked suspicion; resentment; and, in some cases, open hostility. At that time Braille bills were regarded as a condemnation of the education system for blind children and hence were viewed as an attack on professionals in the field of work with the blind.

Today, only five years after passage of the first Braille bill, the mood has changed. In many states parents, educators, and adult blind people are coming together, not to debate whether a Braille bill should be introduced, but to collaborate on the best way to craft the bill. In addition to the requirement that Braille be considered by the IEP team, two other elements have surfaced in more recent Braille bills. One is a requirement for competency testing for teachers of blind children, and the other, which was included in the Texas bill adopted in the summer of '91, requires textbook publishers to make materials available in a machine-readable format for easy translation into Braille.

The stimulus for the introduction of Braille bills was a shared conviction that our nation has produced a generation of virtually illiterate blind children due to the lack of Braille instruction. Many things contributed to this problem, not the least of which was the mainstreaming movement itself. With a nationwide shortage of trained teachers and with children more widely distributed throughout local schools, teachers were faced with the very real problem of choosing print or Braille instruction for a child they were scheduled to see only an hour or two a week. The temptation to favor the print medium, with which they were more familiar, was compounded by a mindset that presumed print reading was superior to Braille. In the 1970's educators came to regard Braille implicitly or explicitly as an antiquated tool for reading. Many felt that new technology would make Braille obsolete, so there was little motivation for teachers to learn the code and even less to teach it.

But a generation of illiterate children has stimulated a counterforce bent on changing this direction before another generation is lost. It is not surprising that we are now hearing a call for better preparation of teachers as well as competency testing to insure that those charged with the education of blind children are themselves competent to provide instruction in Braille reading and writing. Ironically, although fifteen years ago the experts believed that technology would make Braille obsolete, in fact the opposite has proven to be true. With an increased emphasis on Braille, technology has been applied to the problem, the effect being greater availability of Braille than ever before.

It is not surprising that increasing attention has been focused on Braille literacy since literacy generally has become a central topic in America today. The need for blind youngsters to be literate is in many ways self-evident. Literacy for these children, as for sighted ones, is vital to their competing successfully in an increasingly demanding world market. A command of the English language and the ability to read and write are essential to everyone for effective communication. Yet as I prepared for this afternoon's presentation, I had a sense that for me as a blind person the importance of literacy took on a dimension which transcended the readily recognizable importance of being literate. I could not help feeling that the role of Braille in my personal life and its absolute importance to me were somehow connected to the cause-and-effect relationships out-lined earlier, which have resulted in the current emphasis on Braille.

I have a personal and deep-seated loyalty to Braille, not simply because it affords me the ability to read and write. For me Braille is part of my liberation from a debilitating mindset and a body of beliefs premised on the assumption of limitation and hope-lessness. Braille allows me to orga-nize my work, to jot down an address, or to read a recipe; but it also repre-sents the tangible expression of the truth of the principle that, given training and opportunity, blind people can function competitively in society.

When I was seven years old, I be-came legally blind. Over the next nine years my vision gradually de-creased. During this time I was not taught Braille; however, this was also during the period which has come to be known as the sightsaving era. This concept was based on the belief that to use remaining vision would cause it to decrease. For this reason I was not allowed to read print while simultaneously being discouraged from reading Braille. The real tragedy was that as a child I already had deeply ingrained negative attitudes about blindness. I equated it with inferiority and therefore wanted nothing to do with Braille or any other skills which blind people use. As my vision decreased, I fell into a pattern of believing that what I could not see, I could not do. Blindness for me represented helplessness, and my fear of blindness had prevented me from learning the skills which would have allowed me to function. My lack of literacy meant that I had no means by which to read and write, but additionally it contributed to my fundamental feelings of inadequacy and isolation.

After becoming totally blind, I can remember a hospital social worker bringing me a Braille watch. I vividly remember struggling to distinguish the dots on the face of the watch and finding it virtually impossible to distinguish between the hour hand and the minute hand, but in a short time I had managed to learn how to read my watch quickly and accurately and by so doing experienced a sense of exhilaration. While I was not yet truly reading, that experience sparked my recognition that as a blind person I was not entirely helpless—dependent on those around me for even the most basic information. Rather than representing my most negative fears about blindness, Braille started to be a means of liberation. For the first time I began to view my limitations as stemming from my lack of training rather than from my lack of eyesight. For the first time a technique associated with blindness became a source of pride, and I began to understand that perhaps I could function competitively as a blind person using alternative techniques.

While I was in college, I had an experience which represented a milestone in my life. In the Fall of 1974 here in Los Angeles, I attended a convention of the National Federation of the Blind. There I was first exposed to blind people who were living active, normal lives. I met blind people who were holding professional jobs, buying their own homes, and raising families, all of which I had believed were unattainable for me as a blind person. Rather than fitting my preconception of what life as a blind person must be, these men and women were living rich and fulfilling lives, competing effectively in society. These were people I could admire and whom I wished to be like.

A man who stands out in my mind was Lawrence (Muzzy) Marcelino. When I met him, he asked my name, and I can remember his reaching into his pocket and pulling out a slate and stylus to take down my address and phone number. This seemingly small act was nevertheless significant in my life. Muzzy's use of the slate and stylus represented literacy, but it also represented a shaking off of societal stereotypes about blindness. Muzzy believed he could function competitively and so quite naturally put his beliefs into practice. I, on the other hand, was just awakening to the realization that my fears and misconceptions about blindness were driving my actions and hence were primarily responsible for my inability to compete. Braille for me came to represent literacy in my life with all the advantages normally associated with literacy. The element that I regard as most crucial is that Braille also came to symbolize tangible proof of my ability to live a normal life.

The decline in Braille use in our country over the past two decades is nothing less than a tragedy. Children growing up during this period have suffered lost opportunities by having inadequate ability to read and write, compounded by lowered self-esteem and diminished expectations. You in this room have contributed in an important way to reversing this trend, helping blind children reach their true potential through the teaching and producing of Braille. Your efforts have helped many attain literacy and, through it, increased opportunity.

In this room this afternoon is a young woman who grew up in California and received special education services through the public schools. Although she was diagnosed with retinitis pigmentosa, the conventional wisdom of the time indicated that she had too much vision to be taught Braille. By the time she graduated from high school, she was no longer able to read print; yet she had no alternate means of reading and writing. Through ingenuity and hard work she managed to get through college with good grades, while paying a severe price in damaged self-confidence. Fortunately for her, she recognized her need for training. After completing college, she entered the Louisiana Center for the Blind for six months of intensive training in Braille, cane travel, and the other skills of blindness. I remember listening to a presentation she made shortly after completing her training. After having read Braille for only six months, she read Braille faster than she had ever been able to read print. So Braille represented both literacy and freedom to her.

The movement toward increased emphasis on Braille is gathering momentum; and, as with all social change, events are driving other events. To understand the cause-and-effect relationship which has resulted in today's Braille movement, we must first understand that Braille symbolizes both literacy and a change in our own attitudes about blindness. At first glance it seems obvious that two decades of diminished literacy has provided the driving force for today's Braille renaissance. Yet exploring further discloses that the fundamental shift in our attitudes about blindness has made diminished literacy for blind people intolerable. If we expect very little from blind people, then illiteracy, rather than a problem requiring solution, is accepted as a natural situation, consistent with our low expectations.

The Braille movement today is not simply a response to the condition of illiteracy. It is also the outgrowth of the very positive influence of changing social attitudes. With increased expectations for ourselves as blind people, we expand our potential. As we believe we can do more, we naturally look for the tools necessary to translate our beliefs into action. As teachers and producers of Braille, you have seen the effects of your labor in the lives of those with whom you have worked. As your efforts result in increased opportunities, your positive perception of blindness and expectations for blind people are reinforced and expanded.

This change in our conception of blindness gives meaning to the Braille movement. It gives purpose to the new initiatives aimed at greater literacy. The new spirit of cooperation resulting in the adoption of Braille bills, the development of NLS competency testing, and the initiation of ventures with textbook publishers to make Braille more available to school children is directly attributable to this fundamental change in our conceptions. In North America it has led us to undertake a project to study the idea of a unified literary and math code.

We can see the same spirit of co-operation internationally, and I believe it can be explained by the same cause-and-effect relationship between increased expectations and greater emphasis on Braille literacy. The momentum which has developed may well result in a single internationally recognized literary and math code. This same momentum has already brought us to the threshold of an internationally agreed-upon music code.

Throughout this process mistakes will inevitably be made. Bad decisions will be reached which will need to be reviewed and repaired. Some changes will make Braille more awkward and less readable and will perhaps result in real harm to people. Yet the momentum underway brings the promise of true progress. Many years ago I remember being warned,

"If you are not making mistakes, then you are not doing anything." There will be problems as progress is made, yet progress is clearly in evidence.

Braille has allowed me to unlock many doors. It has helped me attain literacy and enabled me to shake off doubt and uncertainty in myself. For this reason I thank you for your role in helping scores of blind children to acquire the tools to reach their full potential. Collectively we are part of the cause and effect relationship stimulating change. Self-confidence and a changing perception of blindness must be nourished by the success which comes from having the ability to put that confidence into action. Your efforts and your dedication have touched countless lives, sustaining the momentum in the cycle of cause and effect, leading us closer to the promise of true integration for the blind.

Claudel Stocker, for many years head of the Braille Development Section of the National Library Service for the Blind and Physically Handicapped, instructs Kevin and Antoinette Hatton in the fine art of using the slate and stylus. The Hatton's son Kevin is blind, and his parents attended this workshop at the convention of the National Federation of the Blind in order to learn how they could help him.

BRAILLE—WHAT IS IT? WHAT DOES IT MEAN TO THE BLIND?

Braille is a system of reading and writing by touch used by the blind. It consists of arrangements of dots which make up letters of the alphabet, numbers, and punctuation marks. The basic Braille symbol, called the Braille cell, consists of six dots arranged in the formation of a rectangle, three dots high and two across. Other symbols consist of only some of these six dots. The six dots are commonly referred to by number according to their position in the cell:

1••4
2••5
3••6

There are no different symbols for capital letters in Braille. Capitalization is accomplished by placing a dot 6 in the cell just before the letter that is capitalized. The first ten letters of the alphabet are used to make numbers. These are preceded by a number sign which is dots 3-4-5-6:

Thus, 1 is number sign a; 2 is number sign b; 10 is number sign a-j and 193 is number sign a-i-c:

Some abbreviations are used in standard American Braille in order to reduce its bulk. These must be memorized, but most Braille readers and writers find them convenient, rather than a problem. Braille is written on heavy paper, and the raised dots prevent the pages from lying smoothly together as they would in a print book. Therefore, Braille books are quite bulky.

Today there are three methods of writing Braille, just as there are two methods of writing print. A Braille writing machine (comparable to a typewriter) has a keyboard of only six keys and a space bar, instead of one key for each letter of the alphabet. These keys can be pushed separately or altogether. If they are all pushed at the same time, they will cause six dots to be raised on the paper in the formation of a Braille cell. Pushing various combinations of the keys on the Braille writer produces different letters of the alphabet and other Braille symbols.

Writing Braille with a slate and stylus compares to writing print with a pen or pencil. The stylus is used to push dots down through the paper, while the slate serves as a guide. The Braille slate can be made of metal or plastic and is hinged so that there is a guide under the paper as well as on top of it. A person writing Braille with the slate and stylus begins at the right side of the paper and ends the line on the left, since the dots are being produced on the underside of the paper. Of course, the Braille reader reads from left to right, for the dots are then on the top side of the paper. Although this may seem a bit confusing, it need not be at all troublesome, since both reading and writing progress through words and sentences from beginning to end in the same manner. The speed of writing Braille with the slate and stylus is about the same as the speed of writing print with pen or pencil.

Just as the personal computer has revolutionized writing in print today, it is also possible to produce Braille more easily and quickly than ever before. Assuming that the proper equipment is available, a computer user can now send a document to a standard printer to produce a paper copy in print or to a Braille embosser to produce the document in Braille. And one need not even know Braille to create this miracle.

Braille was first developed in the late 1820's by a young Frenchman named Louis Braille. He created Braille by modifying a system of night writing which was intended for military use. He did this work as a very young man and had it complete by the time he was about eighteen. He and his friends at the school for the blind found that reading and writing dots was much faster than reading raised print letters, which could not be written by hand at all. The development of this system by young Louis Braille is now recognized as the most important single development in making it possible for the blind to get a good education.

It took more than a century, however, before people would accept Braille as an excellent way for the blind to read and write. Even today many people underestimate the effectiveness of Braille. While tapes and records are enjoyable, Braille is essential for note-taking and helpful for studying such things as math, spelling, and foreign languages. It is a matter of great concern to members of the National Federation of the Blind that fewer blind people now have the opportunity to become good Braille users than did twenty-five years ago.

Why is this? Many professionals in work with the blind stress recorded media with blind children. Many people who become blind do so in old age and are not encouraged to spend the time and make the effort needed to develop the new reading and writing skills that depend on feeling rather than seeing. There are even Braille teachers who do not expect speed and accuracy of their blind students. As a result, the students learn Braille as a chore and a drudgery.

Experienced Braille readers, however, read Braille at speeds comparable to print readers—200 to 400 words a minute. Such Braille readers say that the only limitation of Braille is that there isn't enough material available. They want more books produced by Braille presses, more books produced by volunteer Braillists in their homes, and wider availability of computerized Braille production.

One of the goals of the National Federation of the Blind is to help people appreciate Braille for the efficient system it is. The main difference between print and Braille is simply that print is meant to be read with the eyes, while Braille is meant to be read with the fingertips. Fingers feel dots quickly and accurately; eyes see loops and lines of ink. In both cases it is the brain that processes and reacts to the raw data sent to it by the fingers or the eyes.

This article was first written in Braille and transcribed into print to answer the questions of sighted people who cannot read Braille.

If you have further questions about Braille or blindness, write to the National Federation of the Blind, 1800 Johnson Street, Baltimore, Maryland 21230.

A LUCKY BEGINNING, A HAPPY ENDING

When Betty Niceley was a child in Kentucky, any youngster who could not read print easily for a long time was sent as a matter of course to the Kentucky School for the Blind. Betty's visual acuity was twenty over sixty and was supposed to be stable. She had no trouble reading print, but she could do so for only brief periods without the words blurring.

So it was the residential school for her, and the rule there was that every student was taught Braille, regardless of ability to decode print. Betty remembers that, when Braille books ran short, she was often given print, which worked fine for one class or one assignment. But, if she had to read much, she depended on Braille.

The importance of Braille in her life took on new significance when

Betty Niceley is the President of NAPUB. She works to make Braille available to everyone who needs it.

she was twenty-two. Suddenly and without warning she lost her remaining vision. She had adjustments to make, of course, but learning to read and write over again was not one of them. Betty has made a career for herself teaching the skills of blindness to those just beginning to deal with the disability and administering such programs. She knows firsthand how lucky she was to be taught Braille early because every day she helps people who are dealing with the consequences of not doing so.

Her enthusiastic belief in Braille is the reason she works so hard as the President of the National Association to Promote the Use of Braille (NAPUB). Despite home, family, career, and other work in the National Federation of the Blind, Betty has led NAPUB for more than ten years now—ten years of educating and advocating for improved Braille instruction for blind children today.

In conjunction with the National Organization of Parents of Blind Children, NAPUB sponsors the Braille Readers Are Leaders reading contest annually to encourage blind youngsters to read Braille, and NAPUB members mentor new Braille users and work to inspire them to improve their skills. This work is beginning to bear fruit. Increasingly blind people are advocating for good Braille instruction and using the code themselves, even when they find it slow because they did not learn it as children. A song sung to the tune of "Jingle Bells" expresses what they have come to believe:

Ode to the Code

Going to the school to write an IEP—
The experts say "Choose print because
    your child can see,"
But the equipment is too big, and
    large print is too rare,
And fifteen words a minute will not
    get you anywhere.

Refrain

Braille is here, Braille is here, Braille
is here to stay.
We will keep on using it; we don't care
what you say.
Braille is here, Braille is here, we will
sing its praise.
It's the system for the blind to get a
job that pays!
They say that Braille's too tough to
teach the newly blind.
Its codes and its contractions discom-
bobulate the mind.
But contractions we've learned all,
and codes we've mastered too,
For blindness has no negative effect
on our I.Q.

Refrain

They say that Braille's complex; they
say that it's too slow.
They say the new technology's the
only way to go,
But we'll keep using Braille because
it is the key

To making sure that blind folks will
be literate and free.

Refrain

You can help us spread the word...

...about our Braille Readers Are Leaders contest for blind schoolchildren, a project which encourages blind children to achieve literacy through Braille.

...about our scholarships for deserving blind college students.

...about Job Opportunities for the Blind, a program that matches capable blind people with employers who need their skills.

...about where to turn for accurate information about blindness and the abilities of the blind.

Most importantly, you can help us by sharing what you've learned about blindness in these pages with your family and friends. If you know anyone who needs assistance with the problems of blindness, please write:

Marc Maurer, President
National Federation of the Blind
1800 Johnson Street, Suite 300
Baltimore, Maryland 21230-4998

Other Ways You Can Help the National Federation of the Blind

Write to us for tax-saving information on bequests and planned giving programs.

or

Include the following language in your will:

"I give, devise, and bequeath unto National Federation of the Blind, 1800 Johnson Street, Suite 300, Baltimore, Maryland 21230, a District of Columbia nonprofit corporation, the sum of $___ (or "___ percent of my net estate") to be used for its worthy purposes on behalf of blind persons."

Your contributions are tax-deductible